English G 21

Klassenarbeitstrainer
für Schülerinnen und Schüler

mit Audios und
Lösungen online

 Dein Online-Angebot enthält: Audios und Lösungen.
Du findest alles auf scook.de.
Dort gibst du den unten stehenden Zugangscode
in die Box ein.

Dein Zugangscode auf
www.scook.de | nnfc3-voqzf

English G 21 • Band A 6

Klassenarbeitstrainer mit Lösungen und Lerntipps

Konzeption
Dr. Ursula Mulla und Nogi Mulla, Germering

Erarbeitet von
Martin Kohn, Frankfurt/Main
Bärbel Schweitzer M.A., Staufen

In Zusammenarbeit mit der Englischredaktion
Dr. Christiane Kallenbach (Projektleitung)
Ulrike Berendt (verantwortliche Redakteurin), Doreen Arnold
Susanne Bennetreu, Stefanie Juhnke (Bildredaktion)

Beratende Mitwirkung
Katrin Häntzschel, Wiesa

Tonaufnahmen
Clarity Studio Berlin

Bildquellen
Alamy, Abingdon (S.5 li.: Catchlight Visual Services; S.7 imagebroker; S.12 oben: SuperStock; S.16: ClassicStock; S.18: Rob Watkins; S.23: Pictorial Press Ltd; S.31: Kuttig-People; S.32 oben li.: ACE STOCK LIMITED, oben re.: whiteboxmedia, unten: MARKA; S.48: Lebrecht Music and Arts Photo Library; S.51: Alaska cover girl (M): Itani Images); **Cinetext**, Frankfurt/Main (S.43: Sammlung Richter); **Corbis**, Düsseldorf (S.47: Ocean (RF)); **Getty Images**, München (S.20: NY Daily News); **iStockphoto**, Calgary (S.4: rcaucino; S.5 re.: bloodstone; S.10: zoranm; S.19: alexxx1981; S.22: asiseeit; S.24: Michelle Malven; S.42 li.: georgemuresan, re.: laflor); **Photolibrary**, London (S.51: Cover candle (M)); **Schapowalow**, Hamburg (S.51 cover tulips (M): Zoellner); **Shutterstock**, New York (S.9: Tracy Whiteside; S.12 unten: Daboost; S.14: O Driscoll Imaging; S.25: Digital Genetics; S.26: Kuzmin Andrey; S.29 CREATISTA; S.33: Marty Wakat; S.36: Sarunyu_foto; S.37: Ingrid Balabanova; S.38: Jules_Kitano; S.39: trailexplorers; S.40 li.: cosma, re.: luchschen; S.41: MANDY GODBEHEAR; S.45: Deklofenak; S.55: Jaco Becker; S.56: Dmitry Kalinovsky; S.58: Nikitina Olga)

Textquellen
S.27: Abridged and adapted from "Gang members urged to escape life of violence in new scheme" by Amelia Hill. © Guardian News and Media Ltd 2012; **S.34:** Abridged and adapted from "What's that sound? It's Masternaut, the car gadget that says you're driving badly" by Charles Arthur. © Guardian News and Media Ltd 2012; **S.52–53:** "Ex Poser" from *Unmentionable* by Paul Jennings. Reproduced with permission by Penguin Group (Australia); **S.58:** "What lips my lips have kissed, and where, and why" with special thanks to The Edna St. Vincent Millay Society.

Titelbild
Getty Images, München: (woman (M): Erik Isakson (RF))

Layout und technische Umsetzung
Heike Freund, Hameln

Umschlaggestaltung
Klein & Halm Grafikdesign, Berlin

www.cornelsen.de
www.EnglishG.de

1. Auflage, 4. Druck 2020

© 2012 Cornelsen Schulverlag GmbH, Berlin
© 2019 Cornelsen Verlag GmbH, Berlin

Das Werk und seine Teile sind urheberrechtlich geschützt. Jede Nutzung in anderen als den gesetzlich zugelassenen Fällen bedarf der vorherigen schriftlichen Einwilligung des Verlages.
Hinweis zu §§ 60a, 60b UrhG: Weder das Werk noch seine Teile dürfen ohne eine solche Einwilligung an Schulen oder in Unterrichts- und Lehrmedien (§ 60b Abs. 3 UrhG) vervielfältigt, insbesondere kopiert oder eingescannt, verbreitet oder in ein Netzwerk eingestellt oder sonst öffentlich zugänglich gemacht oder wiedergegeben werden. Dies gilt auch für Intranets von Schulen.

Druck: H. Heenemann, Berlin

ISBN 978-3-06-032940-3

PEFC zertifiziert
Dieses Produkt stammt aus nachhaltig bewirtschafteten Wäldern und kontrollierten Quellen.
www.pefc.de
PEFC/04-31-1156

INHALT

Unit	Klassenarbeit	Seite
Unit 1	**Klassenarbeit A** Listening • Reading • Language • Speaking	5
	Klassenarbeit B Reading • Language • Mediation • Writing	13
Unit 2	**Klassenarbeit A** Listening • Language • Mediation • Study Skills	20
	Klassenarbeit B Listening • Reading • Language • Writing • Speaking	26
Unit 3	**Klassenarbeit A** Listening • Reading • Language • Mediation • Speaking	33
	Klassenarbeit B Listening • Reading • Language • Writing • Study Skills	41
Unit 4	**Klassenarbeit A** Listening • Language • Writing	47
	Klassenarbeit B Reading • Language • Mediation • Speaking	52
Zusatz	**Exam Skills** How to do well in a test	59

Gut vorbereitet ...

... in die nächste Klassenarbeit.

Liebe Schülerin, lieber Schüler,

der vorliegende Klassenarbeitstrainer bietet dir eine ideale Ergänzung für ein effektives Lernen für bevorstehende Klassenarbeiten.

Unterschiedliche Aufgaben zu allen wesentlichen Themen des Lehrwerkes unterstützen dich gezielt bei der Vorbereitung und beim Üben für alle mündlichen und schriftlichen Überprüfungen.

In jeder Unit findest du zwei Klassenarbeiten, mit denen du alle Fertigkeiten (skills) trainieren kannst, die du für die Klassenarbeiten benötigst.

Noch ein paar gute Tipps für deine Arbeit mit dem Klassenarbeitstrainer:

- Erkundige dich bei deiner Lehrerin / deinem Lehrer vorher genau, was in der nächsten Klassenarbeit dran kommt.

- Plane genügend Zeit für die Vorbereitung ein – jeden Tag ein bisschen üben ist effektiver, als am letzten Nachmittag vor der Arbeit alles zu pauken! So kannst du einen scheinbar großen Berg nach und nach erklimmen.

- Die Lösungen zu allen Aufgaben findest du online auf www.scook.de. Gib dazu den Zugangscode von Seite 1 ein. Vergleiche deine Lösungen mit ihnen und gib dir Punkte. Mit dem Punkteschlüssel am Anfang deines Klassenarbeitstrainers kannst du deine Leistung anhand der Gesamtpunktzahl selbst einschätzen.

- Sieh dir deine Fehler genau an und überlege, wie du sie in der Arbeit vermeiden kannst.

Die Klassenarbeiten in diesem Heft prüfen alle Lernbereiche sehr genau ab und können deshalb umfangreicher sein als eine Schulstunde. Sei also nicht verunsichert, wenn du mehr als 45 Minuten für die Bearbeitung benötigst.

Ich wünsche dir nun viel Erfolg und eine Menge Spaß bei der Vorbereitung auf die Klassenarbeiten in diesem Schuljahr.

All the best,

Martin Kohn

Klassenarbeit A

Unit 1

5

Gesamtpunktzahl ohne Speaking ____ / 68   Note ____

Gesamtpunktzahl mit Speaking ____ / 88   Note ____

LISTENING

____ / 24

**A radio phone-in – today's topic:
How did you meet your partner?**

 01 **a)** *Listen to Lisa and Nick. Do the multiple choice tasks and tick the best answer each. (8P)*

1	Lisa talks about	a) her birthday and the day before.	
		b) her 20th birthday.	
		c) a man in her evening classes.	
		d) her birthday presents.	
2	The young man	a) used his credit card.	
		b) didn't want to have the money back.	
		c) was standing behind Lisa.	
		d) wanted to come to Lisa's party.	
3	Lisa and the young man	a) drank a bottle of French wine together.	
		b) started going out after her party.	
		c) want to get married soon.	
		d) want to have at least three children.	
4	The reporter says that	a) he wants to hear more romantic stories.	
		b) there is a break now.	
		c) it was a romantic story.	
		d) they are playing a love song.	
5	Nick fell in love with	a) a girl from his school.	
		b) a pretty girl in his neighbourhood.	
		c) a new girl from London.	
		d) a pretty girl he met on the street.	

Unit 1 | Klassenarbeit A

6	All boys in class fancied her	a) and wrote poems, recorded cassettes, acted cool.	☐
		b) and wrote letters, recorded cassettes, acted stupid.	☐
		c) and wrote letters, recorded cassettes, acted cool.	☐
		d) and wrote love songs, recorded cassettes, acted cool.	☐
7	One day they met	a) at the park.	☐
		b) at a workshop.	☐
		c) at her workplace.	☐
		d) at a shop.	☐
8	They	a) married each other.	☐
		b) married different partners.	☐
		c) never got married.	☐
		d) have been married for ten years.	☐

🎧 02 **b)** Listen to Anna. Complete the sentences. Press 'pause' when Anna has finished. (8P)

1 Anna got to know her boyfriend _____

_____. *(2 facts)*

2 Her cousin lives in Germany, and her husband _____.

3 Anna sat next to _____.

4 The German boy _____.

5 Their conversation got better when they _____.

6 On the day after the wedding party _____.

7 When Anna has finished college, she _____.

🎧 02 **c)** Now listen to Leo. Then say whether the sentences are right or wrong. Tick the correct box and correct the wrong statements. You may listen again. (8P)

		Right	Wrong	Correction
1	Leo had invited a friend to a dancing club.	☐	☐	
2	There were more boys than girls.	☐	☐	
3	Leo talked a lot to the nice girl.	☐	☐	
4	Leo had some problems with dancing.	☐	☐	
5	Perhaps Leo will go to the classes again.	☐	☐	

READING

____/10

Computer games – danger or fun?

1 Violent computer games are the subject of much discussion amongst researchers. Killing games, especially, have become the focus of attention in recent years following several violent acts committed by young people. It seems as if some people start to mix up real life and violent games. While some research groups stress that young people can learn from playing computer games – they say games can teach problem-solving skills as well as different ways of dealing with conflict situations – others fear that violent games make it difficult for young people to deal with negative emotions. They suggest that long periods spent playing violent games can affect a gamer's social skills and make them more ready to use violence.

2 Different studies have been carried out looking at the effects playing violent computer games have on young people; however, they have not come up with clear results yet. Some studies point to higher levels of aggression in young people immediately after they have played games involving shootings and other forms of violence. However, researchers say that the aggressive behaviour seen in gamers involved in the research usually has more than one cause and that computer games cannot be blamed alone.

3 Supporters of computer games consider that they provide a way of focusing aggression and strong emotions. Critics, however, see in some games the danger that violence might be learned or imitated. At the same time, others warn that playing violent games could lead to gamers thinking the kind of violence they see on the computer screen is normal: they can be shocked less easily. This seems to be supported by a study in which two sets of children were shown a series of upsetting images. The first group had just played a violent computer game, the second group had been given a non-violent game to play. The second group reacted with more emotion to the images they were shown than the first group.

4 There are particular worries about "first-person shooter" games. These are killing games which show the action from behind the gun, so from the position of the killer. These games can be highly realistic and the fear of some researchers is that players might begin to identify with the characters in the games. They talk about the possibility of the lines between fiction and reality becoming unclear. Much research is still to be done before the situation surrounding the effects of violent computer games becomes clear. Whatever the results show, it may be difficult to change gamers' habits.

Unit 1 | Klassenarbeit A

> **Unbekannte Wörter erschließen**
> Um einen Text zu erfassen, brauchst du nicht jedes einzelne Wort zu verstehen. Es gibt aber unterschiedliche Möglichkeiten, ihre Bedeutung zu erschließen:
> - In vielen Fällen ist es möglich, die Bedeutung unbekannter Wörter aus dem Zusammenhang zu erschließen, d.h. aus den Wörtern, die vor und nach dem zu erschließenden Wort stehen.
> - Manche Wörter sind auch über die Kenntnis ähnlicher Wörter zu erschließen, z.B. kennst du das Wort „popular". „Popularity" ist das dazugehörige Substantiv und könnte im Textzusammenhang als Beliebtheit erschlossen werden. Allerdings musst du auf sogenannte „false friends" aufpassen. Das sind Wörter, die im Deutschen ähnlich aussehen wie im Englischen, aber trotzdem eine ganz andere Bedeutung haben, z.B. *I become, I will*.
> - In vielen Fällen kannst du die Wörter auch über dir bekannte Wörter aus einer anderen Sprache erschließen, z.B. aus dem Französischen *historique, la politique*.
> - Oft wird die Bedeutung von Schlüsselwörtern des Textes durch beigefügte Bilder klar.

a) Read the text. Then match the headings A–E to the paragraphs 1–4. Be careful: there is one more heading than you need. (4P)

- **A** Influencing emotional life
- **B** Real life as a violent game?
- **C** Playing video games leads to aggression
- **D** The connection between aggression and playing games
- **E** Losing touch with reality

1 ☐   2 ☐   3 ☐   4 ☐

b) Decide if the statements are **true**, **false** or **not given**. Tick the correct box. (6P)

		True	False	Not given
1	Some researchers claim that violent computer games prepare people for social problems.	☐	☐	☐
2	Researchers say that through violent computer games gamers learn how to deal with both conflict situations and negative emotions.	☐	☐	☐
3	Playing violent computer games influences relationships to other people.	☐	☐	☐
4	Playing computer games regularly leads to higher levels of aggression.	☐	☐	☐
5	Playing violent computer games doesn't influence the emotions of the people playing.	☐	☐	☐
6	Some researchers claim that it's very likely that people playing killing games identify with the killer.	☐	☐	☐

Unit 1 | Klassenarbeit A

LANGUAGE

____ / 34

1 WORDS Be close, but not too much!

____ / 6

Complete the sentences with words from Unit 1.

1 If you're _____, you always want to be very close to your girlfriend or boyfriend.

2 If you've just got together with someone, it is quite normal to feel _____ about his/her feelings for you.

3 If you break up with someone, you _____ him/her.

4 In a good relationship, you should be faithful and never _____ each other.

5 Girls usually pay more attention to other people's feelings than boys. They are more _____.

6 She felt _____ about not staying at home with her boyfriend but meeting friends.

2 WORDS What does that mean?

____ / 5

Explain the following new words from Unit 1.

1 symptom: _____

2 counsellor: _____

3 evaluation: _____

4 down-to-earth: _____

5 addiction: _____

3 WORDS It's absolutely true

____/7

Complete the sentences with adverbs from the box. Be careful: one of the adverbs has to be used twice.

> certainly • fortunately • hopefully • mostly • partly • unfortunately

1 Boys are the minority among Tom's friends. His friends are _____ girls.

2 Mike is happy: _____, he has time to meet Tom this afternoon.

3 Mike and Sally broke up some weeks ago. _____, Mike hasn't got over her yet.

4 Mike is afraid of calling Sally, _____ because he still feels guilty about breaking up with her and _____ because she might have a new boyfriend.

5 However, Mike decides to call Sally – _____ she doesn't have a boyfriend yet.

6 It's for sure: Mike will _____ try to get Sally back.

4 GRAMMAR What a first date should be like

____/7

Mike has thought much about dating rules and love recently. Circle the correct translation of the German word "sollen".

Old people often think that boys **are supposed to** / **are said to** pay for the first date – I don't think so. The first date **ought to** / **is said to** be very important for the future relationship. So during your first date, you **should** / **are said to** try to find things you are both interested in. You **had better not** / **aren't said to** make too many jokes during the first date but try to listen carefully and remember what she tells you. You **had better not** / **aren't said to** talk about other girls you fancied. I did that once and my date immediately left. If you like the girl after the first date, you **should** / **are supposed to** ask her out again. First love **had better** / **is said to** never be forgotten. So be careful and choose the right girl for your first love!

5 GRAMMAR Yesterday – today – tomorrow

____/9

Write down complete sentences with the correct **modals and their substitutes**.

1 Oliver – play football – when young   (konnte)

_____

2 Now – Oliver – go to school   (muss)

_____

3 In two years – Oliver – work long hours   (wird müssen)

_____

4 Leon – work – as a child   (musste nicht)

_____

5 Today – Leon – do the washing-up   (muss)

_____

6 Leon – buy dishwasher – when own flat   (wird können)

_____

7 Catherine – go dancing – when 15   (durfte nicht)

_____

8 Catherine – stay – at the disco – until 10 p.m.   (darf)

_____

9 Catherine – stay out – as long as she wants – when 21   (wird dürfen)

_____

> **Modale Hilfsverben können nicht alle Zeiten ausbilden, deshalb gibt es Ersatzverben.**
>
> | | Present | Past | Future |
> | --- | --- | --- | --- |
> | *können* | can / am / is / are able to | could / was / were able to | will / won't be able to |
> | *dürfen* | may / can / am / is / are allowed to | could / was / were allowed to | will / won't be allowed to |
> | *müssen* | must / needn't have / has to / don't / doesn't have to | had to / didn't have to | will / won't have to |
>
> Weitere Hilfe findest du im Grammar File 5.2 auf S.178 in deinem Englischbuch.

SPEAKING

____ / 20

Dangers on the net

Have a look at the advert and talk about
- what the advert shows,
- the style,
- the target group,
- the language,
- the message,
- your opinion about the advert.

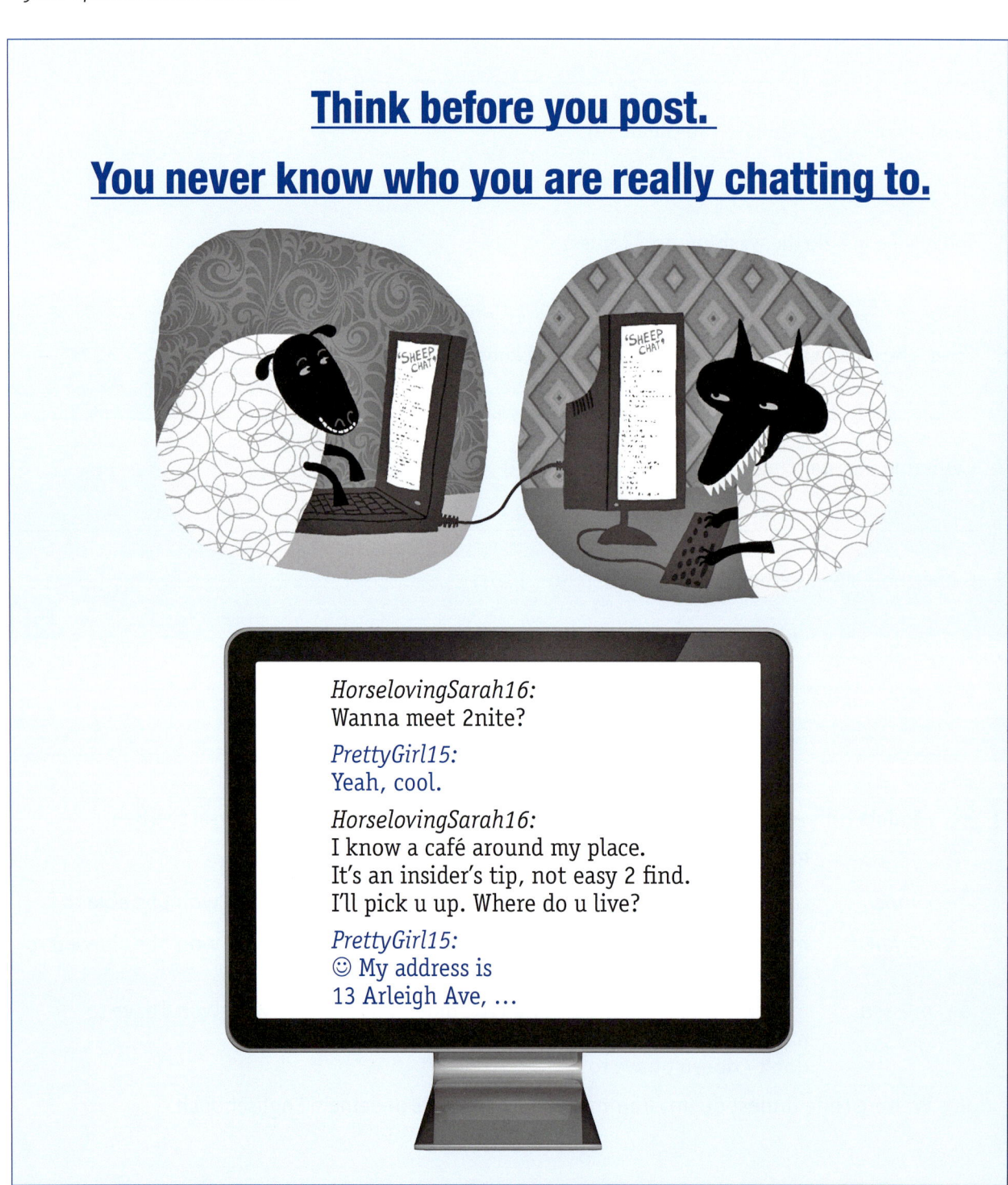

Klassenarbeit B — Unit 1

Gesamtpunktzahl _____ /78   Note _____

READING   _____ /15

Bullies[1] on the net

"They started bullying me when I was 12," says Kerry Finnegan, who is now aged 15. "At first they would call me names in the school yard and one of the girls hit me in the face one day after school. Then it started online. They created a social network group called 'I hate Kerry Finnegan' and wrote messages about the way I look, saying I was fat and ugly and things like that."

Cyber-bullying, like that experienced by Kerry, is quite a new problem in schools, but it is a serious problem and one that is becoming worse. Today more and more communication takes place via the internet, so it is not surprising that bullying takes place online as well.

Cyber-bulling can take different forms. Victims receive messages from bullies by email, text message or through internet chats. Social networking sites are also used by bullies to attack their victims. Photographs of the victim are manipulated in cruel ways. Often the bullies are anonymous, so the victim alone is unable to do anything to stop them.

Studies show that more than half of all cyber-bullies are a classmate of the victim and one in ten is an online friend.

Bullying has always gone on in schools. What is new with cyber-bullying is that it goes beyond the school gates. The comments and jokes follow the victim home and into his or her bedroom when they log into their email or social network account in the evening.

If you are a victim of cyber-bullying, tell your parents or someone you trust immediately what is happening. Don't answer any messages you receive. If the bullying takes place on a social network or in a chatroom, you should contact the platform's operator and ask them to remove the material. They may be able to block the bully from the site. If the situation gets out of control, the law is there to help you, so you can go to the police. Whatever happens, don't keep the bullying to yourself – that's what the bully wants and if you do so, he or she wins.

After being bullied online for more than a year, Kerry talked to her parents about what was happening. They were shocked and contacted Kerry's class teacher, who didn't know what was happening either. The bullies were punished and Kerry closed her social network account and changed her email address and her phone number. Today she uses her experience to help support younger pupils at her school who are victims of bullying.

[1] bully ['bʊli] *Tyrann*

Unit 1 | Klassenarbeit B

a) *Read the text carefully. Answer the questions with information from the text. You don't have to write complete sentences.* (11P)

1 What happens to victims of cyber-bullying? *(3 things)*

   _____

2 What makes it so difficult to do something about cyber-bullying?

   _____

3 What is new with cyber-bullying?

   _____

4 What can you do if you are a victim of cyber-bullying? *(3 things)*

   _____

5 What did Kerry do about being bullied online? *(3 things)*

   _____

b) *Match the sentence halves. Be careful: there is one more phrase than you need.* (4P)

1	Cyber-bullying is a very serious problem	A	but they should tell their parents.
2	Victims cannot usually react directly if they are being bullied	B	but they are often classmates.
3	Victims can be attacked 24 hours a day	C	because the internet can be used anywhere at any time.
4	Victims shouldn't keep the bullying to themselves	D	because the victim can't escape, not even at home.
		E	because they don't know who the bullies are.

| 1 | | 2 | | 3 | | 4 | |

LANGUAGE

____ / 37

1 WORDS Good ≠ bad, bad = awful

____ / 18

a) *Complete the crossword with the correct antonyms and synonyms from Unit 1. (14P)*

Across

1. Synonym of *however*
5. Synonym of *right*
6. Synonym of *(to) see*
7. Synonym of *(to) understand* (2 words)
10. Antonym of *pleasant*
12. Antonym of *(to) raise*
13. Antonym of *written*
14. Antonym of *true*

Down

2. Synonym of *particularly*
3. Antonym of *(to) slow down* (2 words)
4. Synonym of *(to) promise*
8. Synonym of *later*
9. Synonym of *thing*
11. Antonym of *(to) be sure*

b) *Choose four words from the crossword and write a sentence for each one. (4P)*

_____

_____

_____

_____

_____

_____

_____

2 WORDS Teenagers' lives   ____/10

Olivia is collecting some arguments about teenagers' lives today in comparison to the past for a school presentation. Unfortunately, she has made some mistakes and used false friends while taking notes.

Correct the words crossed out.

1. In the past the whole family ate ~~fast~~ every meal together.

   _____

2. Teenagers always helped their parents with the ~~homework~~.

   _____

3. Today most teenagers ~~must not~~ help at home.

   _____

4. Teachers had a different ~~meaning~~ about education.

   _____

5. Today many teenagers ~~become~~ the chance to go abroad.

   _____

6. Today some parents ~~wonder~~ to hear how their child behaves at school.

   _____

7. They cannot believe that their child has ~~got~~ so rude.

   _____

8. Older people often ~~mean~~ that teenagers are lazy.

   _____

9. The ~~ground~~ for this is that teenagers today have more leisure time and more opportunities.

   _____

10. It's a ~~failure~~ to think that there are fewer rules for teenagers.

    _____

3 GRAMMAR I have the date!

___ / 9

Sophie wrote an entry into her diary about a boy she fancies. Unfortunately, she has forgotten to put in the adverbs. Fill in the adverbs at the correct position.

> **Satzstellung von Adverbien**
> Beachte bei der Stellung von Adverbien im Satz die folgenden Regeln:
> a) **Satzadverbien** (z. B. *unfortunately, luckily, maybe, finally*) beziehen sich auf den gesamten Satz und stehen daher in der Regel am Satzanfang;
> b) **Adverbien der unbestimmten Zeit oder Häufigkeit** (z. B. *already, always, ever, just*) stehen normalerweise vor dem Vollverb;
> c) **Adverbien der Art und Weise** (z. B. *clearly, well*), **Ortsangaben** (z. B. *outside, on the roof*) und **Zeitangaben** (z. B. *tomorrow, a year ago*) stehen gewöhnlich nach dem Vollverb (+ Objekt);
> d) **Gradadverbien** (z. B. *very, quite, too, really*) stehen meist unmittelbar vor dem Wort, auf das sie sich beziehen.

Dear Diary,

I talked to this cool, handsome guy from my school today. (finally)

_____

He stood next to me when I was waiting to have lunch in the cafeteria. (suddenly)

_____

I ran away because I was so excited. (almost)

_____

I started a conversation with him. (at last)

_____

We had a nice chat and he told me that he had been ice skating before. (never)

_____

That was my chance! (really)

_____

Although I'm shy, I asked him out at the weekend. (very)

_____

I couldn't believe it, but he accepted! (at first)

_____

I'm nervous about my first date with him! (quite)

_____

I'll write more tomorrow. Good night.

Unit 1 | Klassenarbeit B

MEDIATION

____ / 14

Swamp[1] football

It's project week at your school. You are in the group "fun sports of the world". Everybody has to give a short presentation on the open day. The new exchange student in class, Mika from Finland, wants to present swamp football. As he feels unsure about presenting in German, you agreed to help him.

Listen to Mika's presentation and tell the audience in German what he is talking about.

Press "pause" when you hear the beep. Press "play" when you've said your part.

> **Mediation**
> Du musst bei Mediation nicht wortwörtlich ins Deutsche übersetzen, aber genau zuhören und dann sinngemäß das Wesentliche ins Deutsche übertragen.

[1] swamp [swɒmp] *Sumpf*

WRITING

____/12

Men and women ...

Read the statement and discuss why you agree or disagree with it. Write about 250 words.

I can't believe this idiot broke up with me. So my aunt is right: men and women just don't go together.

> **☞ Discussing a statement**
> - Bevor du mit dem Schreiben beginnst, sammle Argumente für und gegen die These. Das kannst du z. B. in einer Mindmap machen.
> - Dein Text braucht eine Einleitung, in der du die These erklärst. Dann präsentierst du deine Argumente dafür und dagegen und gibst Beispiele und Belege.
> - Beende deinen Text mit deiner eigenen Meinung.

Unit 2 — Klassenarbeit A

Gesamtpunktzahl _____ / 81   Note _____

LISTENING

_____ / 10

🎧 04 **Women's Rights Are Human Rights**

Listen to this famous speech which was originally given by the former First Lady of the USA, Hillary Rodham Clinton, in Beijing in China on September 5th, 1995.

a) *Complete the sentences.* (5P)

1 Women come together _____.

2 When women come together _____.

3 However different women may appear, _____
   _____.

4 Let us create a world _____.

5 Every family _____.

b) *Are the following statements right or wrong? Correct the wrong sentences.* (5P)

Clinton says …

1 Women are educated all over the world.
   _____
   _____

2 Women share a common future.
   _____
   _____

3 A world should be created where all women treat men with respect.
   _____
   _____

4 If women are treated equally, this leads to healthy families, and healthy families lead to healthy communities.
   _____

5 Women's lives can't get better.
   _____
   _____

Unit 2 | Klassenarbeit A   21

LANGUAGE

____ / 42

1   WORDS Volunteer work

____ / 11

a) *Circle the correct word in the text. (8P)*

> I am a volunteer in **an offensive** / **a humanitarian** organization. This organization **challenges** / **stands up** and fights for people's rights all over the world. One of its main aims is the fight against **torture** / **sympathy**. Fair **treatment** / **agreement** must be available to everybody. Another very important aim is the fight against **xenophobic** / **significant** behaviour. It's important to talk to people and convince them that we all have the same rights. We all need to **communicate** / **be silent** with each other to influence things. I **contribute** / **am convinced** that I can do a lot to help people in my **district** / **brotherhood**.

b) *Choose **three** words that you didn't need in the text and write a sentence for each one. (3P)*

_____

_____

_____

2   GRAMMAR Activity and state verbs

____ / 8

a) *Complete the sentences with the correct form of the verb in brackets. Use the **progressive form** whenever both **simple present** and **present progressive** are possible. (6P)*

1 We _____ (believe) that everybody can help to make a change.

2 You only _____ (need) to stand up and fight for your rights.

3 It's important to know what is happening in the world. That's why I _____ (read) the newspaper.

4 I _____ (not think) you should do this! –

   Nevertheless, I _____ (think) about it.

5 My grandmother _____ (remember) the demonstrations for human rights in the sixties.

b) *Translate sentence number **four** into German. (2P)*

_____

_____

3 GRAMMAR The importance of voting

___ / 5

*Re-write the sentences to put special emphasis on the words underlined either by changing the **word order**, by using an **emphasizing -self pronoun** or by using **emphatic do/does/did**.*

By voting, you can make a change if you want it.

By voting, you yourself can make a change if you want it.

1 Democracy gives you the chance to take part in elections.

___

2 Democracy, not absolute monarchy, gives people the chance to influence political decisions.

___

3 You should never miss a vote just because you are dissatisfied.

___

4 The one who can influence politics is you.

___

5 An election has rarely attracted so much media attention.

___

4 GRAMMAR The right to vote

___ / 18

Erin wrote two texts about the right to vote, but he is unsure which tenses he should use. Circle the correct form of the verb.

a) *First he wrote about the current situation. Use the **simple present** or **present progressive**. (10P)*

> Every now and then, politicians in Germany **discuss / are discussing** at what age teenagers should have the right to vote. At the moment we **do / are doing** a project at school where we **ask / are asking** our fellow students whether they **learn / are learning** enough about politics at school to be able to vote at 16. It is interesting to get teenagers' opinions about their role in politics. While some of the students **say / are saying** that they would rather have fun with their friends than listen to political discussions, others **see / are seeing** their responsibility and their chance to influence their future. Some students **form / are forming** political groups which **fight / are fighting** for teenagers' right to vote at the age of 16. One group **talks / is talking** to the mayor of our town right now. I think they **try / are trying** to convince him to put that issue on the political agenda at this very moment.

b) *Next he wrote about the history of women's right to vote. Use the **simple past** or **past progressive**. (8P)*

> That reminds me of women in the past who **fought / were fighting** for their right to vote too. While their husbands **discussed / were discussing** political issues and **tried / were trying** to influence their government, the women **took care / were taking care** of their children and the household. However, around the turn of the century women **started / were starting** to fight for the right to vote across Europe. In many countries women **got / were getting** the right to vote at the beginning of the 20th century.
> While in Germany their fight **ended / was ending** successfully in 1918, in England they only **got / were getting** the right in 1928.

MEDIATION

___/15

What young people in Britain are allowed to do

You are going on a class trip to England. Your parents would like to know about the drinking laws in the UK. You have found this text on the web and want to give them the necessary information about it.

Write the information for them in German in your exercise book.

In the UK, children under five must not be given any alcohol unless supervised or ordered by a doctor in an emergency.

If you want to buy alcohol, you have to be at least 18 years old. If you are between 16 and 17, you may consume wine, beer or cider on licensed premises, but only if you have a meal there too. In England and Wales, these drinks must be ordered by an adult. In Scotland, you do not have to be accompanied when you order alcohol at a restaurant and you are older than 16.

In order to be allowed to buy alcohol in the supermarket, you have to be 18. If you want to buy chocolates filled with spirits or liqueur, you need to be 16 years old. This, however, is very rarely checked by the cashiers.

You need to be aware that you might be asked for ID if you look younger than 21 and want to buy alcohol. In many shops and supermarkets, you will find a sign that informs you of this. If you fail to show any ID, you won't be allowed to buy alcohol, even if you are in fact older than 18.

Supermarkets and shops which are found to be selling alcohol to minors can lose their licence to sell alcohol.

STUDY SKILLS

___/14

How to analyse English films

Sam is a member of the film group at his school. For beginners he has written a "how to"-guide about analysing English films.

Complete the sentences with words from the box. Make sure you use the correct form of the words.

> (to) analyse • camera angle • camera work • character • documentary •
> eye-level • feature film • moving picture • science-fiction movie •
> setting • shot • special effect • subtitle • thriller

Sometimes it can be difficult to follow an English film. That is why you should try to find out as much information as you can about the film before watching it.

Before you start analysing a film, you should consider what genre it is. There are _____,

which are stories with sound and _____, and there are _____.

Examples of feature films are westerns, _____, _____

and melodramas. If the film is in a foreign language, either it is dubbed or there are

_____.

Films can be seen as a form of literature, which is why we can _____ films as we do books.

So when you analyse a film, you have to consider its plot, _____, atmosphere and

_____. Characters in films are called the cast. The sound and music, lighting and

camera work are all very important in films. _____ make action movies very exciting.

The _____ can influence the atmosphere of a film and presents the characters in a

certain way. A certain _____ focuses the audience's attention and shows them

what to concentrate on in a scene. There are different types of camera angles: low-angle,

_____ and high-angle shots.

The camera movement leads from close to long

_____.

Keeping a viewing log, in which you note down

the plot, important scenes and your feelings or

impressions while watching, can help you

analyse the whole film at the end.

Unit 2 — Klassenarbeit B

Gesamtpunktzahl ohne Speaking ____/61 Note ____

Gesamtpunktzahl mit Speaking ____/77 Note ____

LISTENING ____/10

🎧 05 **A radio show: The Brave People's Award**

Listen to the radio show. Answer the following questions in a few words.

1. What do many people do when they see something bad happening on the streets?

2. What idea does the Brave People's Award want to promote?

3. How did the girl react to the man coming closer? *(2 facts)*

4. Besides Michael, did anyone else do anything to help the girl?

5. What is the safest way to do something about crime?

6. Why doesn't the girl want her name to be given?

7. What plans of her classmates did the girl hear?

8. Why did she talk to her head teacher about it?

9. What did the head teacher do?

READING

___/21

A new chance?

Read this article from "The Guardian" about how London deals with violent gang members.

Gang members urged[1] to escape life of violence in new scheme

Programme used in Boston and Glasgow, which makes gang members listen to bereaved[2] parents, is started in London

Amelia Hill

guardian.co.uk, Tuesday 31 January 2012 17.30 GMT

Article history

A programme to persuade young gang members to give up lives of street violence has been started in London.

Enfield is the first council[3] in England and Wales to turn to the innovative "call-in" process to deal with its gang problem. The scheme aims to give young known gang members a stark warning about street violence and criminality by making them listen to parents who have lost their children in gang-related violence, to ex-gang members, community leaders and to doctors forced to choose between saving the life of an elderly heart-attack victim or that of a young, badly injured gangster.

The scheme was first tried in Boston in the US and then delivered in Glasgow as part of the Community Initiative to Reduce Violence project.

"In common with many parts of London, Enfield has some problems with gangs, but we are saying 'this ends now' and we'll be leaving the members of these gangs in absolutely no doubt what awaits them if they continue with their current behaviour," said Christine Hamilton, Enfield council's cabinet member for community well-being and public health.

"We want to do everything that we can to encourage these young people to change their behaviour and play an active and productive part in society, but we won't wait to track them down and to punish those responsible for serious anti-social behaviour and criminality."

At the end of the session, the young people are told about the agencies able to help them escape from gang life.

William Graham, who helped Strathclyde police set up the initial "call-in" sessions and advised Enfield council, said the scheme guaranteed that "those that want to get out are helped [while] those that don't will be addressed by the police and put away".

"The call-in basically tells these young people that if you remain in a gang, you will end up in prison or dead – but, as well as giving them a stark warning, it also offers a way out to those who want it," said Graham. "So, the whole gang can be addressed and not only an individual. This has worked very successfully in Glasgow."

The risk of becoming a crime victim in Britain today is at a 30-year low, but this summer's riots in several English cities put gangs back in the headlines and on the political agenda.

The Metropolitan police said that at least half of the 27 murders of teenagers in London in 2007 were gang-related. Officers in Liverpool and Manchester have said in the past that 60% of shootings are linked to gangs.

The government recently introduced so-called "gang injunctions[4]" in England and Wales to limit the movements of people suspected of being gang members. Similar to antisocial behaviour orders, the new powers are also designed to protect the individual by forcing them into a mentoring programme and can be used to ban people from wearing certain colours used by gangs to show membership.

© Guardian News & Media Ltd 2012

---

[1] (to) urge [ɜːdʒ] *dringend bitten* [2] bereaved [bɪˈriːvd] *hinterblieben* [3] council [ˈkaʊnsl] *Kommune*
[4] injunction [ɪnˈdʒʌŋkʃn] *Unterlassungsverfügung*

Unit 2 | Klassenarbeit B

a) Describe in **three** sentences what the text is about. (3P)

_____

_____

_____

b) Read the text again. Then decide if the statements are **true**, **false** or **not given**. (8P)

		True	False	Not given
1	The scheme aims to help victims of gang attacks.	☐	☐	☐
2	Gang members are shown what effect their behaviour has on other people's lives.	☐	☐	☐
3	Enfield is the first council in England and Wales to try the new scheme because it is the most dangerous part of London.	☐	☐	☐
4	Gang members have to take part in social programmes to become an active and productive part in society.	☐	☐	☐
5	The "call-in" shows gang members how to get out of their dangerous lives.	☐	☐	☐
6	At the moment society is being threatened by more and more gangs.	☐	☐	☐
7	50 % of murders in London are related to gangs.	☐	☐	☐
8	Gang members are shown the future they can expect if they don't change their lives.	☐	☐	☐

c) What do you think about such a call-in process as described in the text?
Write a comment of about 120 words in your exercise book. (10P)

 Einen Kurzkommentar schreiben
In einem Kurzkommentar beziehst du Stellung zu einem Zitat oder Text oder einer (manchmal provokanten) These. Es geht nicht darum zu erraten, was deine Lehrerin oder dein Lehrer gern hören möchte – **deine eigene Meinung** ist gefragt!
- Überlege dir, welche **Position** du vertreten möchtest.
- Diskutiere das **Für und Wider: On the one hand …, on the other hand …**
- Schreibe auch zu kurzen Texten eine **Einleitung** und einen zusammenfassenden **Schlusssatz**.

LANGUAGE

___/21

1 WORDS Calming people down with words

___/7

In a conflict, these sentences are not very clever, but rather provocative.
Re-write them keeping their meaning but using the language of de-escalation to calm people down.

1 Your opinion is the worst I have ever heard.
   _____

2 I don't care if I was wrong.
   _____

3 How often do I have to explain this to you?
   _____

4 It's your fault I bumped into you.
   _____

5 I only took your pen, so why are you so annoyed about it?
   _____

6 Don't shout at me.
   _____

7 Watch out, will you!
   _____

Unit 2 | Klassenarbeit B

2 WORDS What does it mean? ___/8

Sometimes you might not know how to say something in English. Then you can explain it in other words. Complete the table either by writing the explanation of the word or by writing the word from Unit 2 that is explained. Give the infinitives of the verbs.

Word	Explanation
	Someone who watches something but doesn't get involved is called a …
	When someone … a crime, he/she should tell the police all about it.
injustice	
	When you think that something is true but don't have proof of it, you … it.
(to) attend	
	If you get harmed in a car accident, you are …
	In a group there are many … members.
expense	

3 GRAMMAR Remembering the past ___/6

*Re-write the following sentences by using **used to + infinitive**. Make sure you use the correct tenses.*

1 In our town – there be fights – between different gangs

_____

2 my grandfather – help poor people – by giving them food

_____

3 Paul – wear glasses – when be at kindergarten

_____

4 my father – work in a bank – before become a teacher

_____

5 Brian – have a car – before the accident

_____

6 Lucy – like Maths – when be at school

_____

WRITING

____/9

Violence after school

Imagine you witnessed the fight in the photo. Write an objective report about the incident for your school magazine in English. Write about 100 words in your exercise book.

 Writing a report
- Finde eine Überschrift.
- Erwähne in einem einleitenden, **zusammenfassenden Satz**, was passiert ist.
- Nenne erst die wichtigen Informationen und anschließend die Details. Dabei kannst du dich an den **Wh-Fragen (Who? What? Where? When? Why?)** orientieren.
- Schreibe deinen Bericht in der Vergangenheit, ohne reißerische Adjektive oder direkte Rede. Es geht lediglich um eine **nüchterne und sachliche Darstellung von Fakten**. Schildere das Geschehen, ohne es zu kommentieren.

SPEAKING

___/ 16

Getting involved

Your English teacher gave you three photos showing people in different situations.
He asked you to prepare a talk about how people can get involved.

> In your talk you should
> - describe what is happening in the photos,
> - choose one photo and say why you would prefer to help in this situation than in the others,
> - explain what you would do if you were watching the scene you have chosen.

Klassenarbeit A

Unit 3

33

Gesamtpunktzahl ohne Speaking ____ / 62   Note _____

Gesamtpunktzahl mit Speaking ____ / 74   Note _____

LISTENING   ____ / 10

🎧 06 **A radio report: Imitating nature**

Listen to a radio report about how we can learn from nature and complete the sentences.

1 Nature is used as _____.

2 One example is gas lines which carry gas up from below the ground. This is similar to the way

   _____.

3 Waterproof clothing was influenced by the way in which _____

   _____.

4 The new study field is called biomimetics, and National Biomimetic Research is a company ____

   _____.

5 Material similar to dolphin skin is used to _____.

6 Ultrasound technologies were influenced by the way _____

   _____.

7 Birds and fish demonstrate _____.

8 'School' is also the term for a _____.

9 We're copying nature _____ and to make

   _____ in the future.

READING

____/ 10

Masternaut

Read the article about a new car system taken from "The Guardian".

What's that sound? It's Masternaut, the car gadget[1] that says you're driving badly

**It isn't an autopilot, and the driverless car is still miles off the garage.
But it could save you a packet on petrol.**

By Charles Arthur

As I turned the wheel to steer the car through the roundabout[2], there was a shriek and the flash of warning lights. Beside me, Wayne Gilbert, chief technology officer at Masternaut, smiled.

I had obviously steered too aggressively into the curve. The lights and the noise came from Masternaut, a new electronic instrument attached to the instrument board that is claimed to encourage more careful and considerate driving – and to cut fuel bills by up to a fifth. When businesses have to explain every expense, and with fuel costs up 46% in real terms in the past five years, that is not an unimportant saving. [...]

An autopilot it is not, yet. Today, it's more like a driving instructor that tells you when you're doing things wrong – stopping too aggressively, speeding up too quickly, or turning so tightly that things might be thrown around in the back. Fit it to a car which is transporting porcelain and you'll see how useful it could be.

Other settings mean it can note when a vehicle[3] hasn't been driven for longer than a set time, a common cause of both pollution and excess[4] fuel use. It's like a super-tachometer, able to locate you on a map and point out where you did things wrong, or right.

In the long term, says Gilbert, we'll see far more advanced feedback between drivers and vehicles. [...] He points to the crash involving 34 vehicles on the M5 in November, when seven people died in a collision suspected of being caused by smoke from a fire. With the technology he expects, the vehicles could have sensed the changing situation on the road and given the drivers more rapid feedback – and perhaps controlled their speed as the car radar noted stopped vehicles on the road ahead.

Automatic stopping systems are already fitted to new Mercedes to prevent the classic 'roundabout accident', where drivers start forward because they see a gap in traffic – but don't realize the motorist in front hasn't moved.

It's not a big step from that to the 'driverless car', an idea for which Google has already applied for a patent. That would create vehicles able, for example, to guide people around tourist spots or find their way to repair shops. It, too, would be based on a GPS locator that would connect to the internet and figure out its location. Google admitted in late 2010 that it had been working on driverless cars when it said test vehicles had gone more than 1,000 miles in the US without drivers, although two humans were always in the car in case the software failed.

Google's engineers say robotic cars will have faster reactions than humans, which could reduce accidents and allow more vehicles into the same road space at any given speed, cutting delays.

The completely driverless car is likely to be some way off, which means systems such as Masternaut's, which is being fitted in cars in the UK and Europe, will become more common. [...]

Gilbert knows his company's systems can help to guarantee careful behaviour: he has two sons. "I told each one, when I let them take my car out, that I'd know precisely how they'd driven it because of the feedback. I told one that if he managed five years without a crash or any points on his licence then I'd buy him a car of his own."

Gilbert had to pay.

© Guardian News & Media Ltd 2012

---

[1] gadget ['gædʒɪt] *Gerät*   [2] roundabout ['raʊndəbaʊt] *Kreisverkehr*   [3] vehicle ['viːəkl] *Fahrzeug*
[4] excess ['ekses] *übermäßig*

a) *Answer the questions in your own words. Write complete sentences. (5P)*

1 What is special about Masternaut?
   _____

2 What is the problem at roundabouts?
   _____

3 What has Google been planning for the last few years?
   _____

4 What might happen to the number of accidents with the help of Masternaut in the future?
   _____

5 What is the advantage of the Masternaut system for parents?
   _____

b) *Read the text again. Do the multiple choice tasks and tick the correct answer. (5P)*

1	Masternaut is like a supertachometer that …	a) gives you feedback about how you are doing.	☐
		b) increases the speed of your car.	☐
		c) knows where the nearest petrol station can be found.	☐

2	The technology of Masternaut can …	a) help drivers to reduce their fuel bills.	☐
		b) help drivers to react faster to the situation on the road.	☐
		c) help drivers to go through traffic more quickly.	☐

3	In new Mercedes cars …	a) automatic stopping systems will be included.	☐
		b) automatic stopping systems didn't work.	☐
		c) automatic stopping systems are already included.	☐

4	There have already been cars without drivers on US streets, but …	a) their software failed.	☐
		b) they caused more accidents than humans did.	☐
		c) there have always been two humans on board in case the software breaks down.	☐

5	Robotic cars …	a) will never be possible.	☐
		b) will be able to react quicker than humans.	☐
		c) will cause more accidents.	☐

LANGUAGE

____/ 27

1 WORDS Science can be breathtaking

____/ 5

Complete the sentences with a compound noun. For each compound noun choose two words from the box. Be careful: each word can be used only once. Pay attention to the spelling.

air • bulb • conditioning • country • developing • earth • light • power • quakes • solar

1 Thomas Alva Edison is known as the inventor of the

   _____.

2 In the summer, _____ is a

   great invention to keep your house cool.

3 _____ uses the sun

   to produce energy.

4 Science can save lives! Experts are working on a new

   technology which will warn people about _____.

5 Especially people in a _____ need more help to cure diseases.

2 WORDS In our world

____/ 7

Complete the table either by writing the explanation of the word or by writing the word that is explained from Unit 3. Give the infinitives of the verbs.

Word	Explanation
	Things that can be broken easily are …
	If something has an influence, it … something.
disgusting	
	Oil is an example of …
freezer	
appropriate	
	You have to … your television if you want to watch it.

3 GRAMMAR Inventions and the environment

___ /7

*Change the sentences into the **passive** and use the words underlined as the subject.*
Make sure you use the correct tenses.

> **The passive**
> Das Passiv bildest du mit einer Form von **to be** und der dritten Form des Verbs (**past participle**). Du kannst damit über Handlungen sprechen, ohne zu sagen, wer diese Handlung ausführt. Möchtest du den „Verursacher" der Handlung nennen, verwendest du die Präposition **by**.
>
> Wenn du weitere Hilfe benötigst, dann sieh im Grammar File 3 auf S. 175–176 in deinem Englischbuch nach.

Yesterday, politicians introduced a new environmental programme.
Yesterday, a new environmental programme was introduced by politicians.

1 Scientists hadn't thought about consequences for the environment before they invented the car.

2 Forty years ago, people did not talk so much about pollution.

3 Now scientists are developing new technologies.

4 They have even produced fast electric cars.

5 But a lot of cars still emit a lot of CO_2 gases into the air.

6 Governments must reduce car and factory emissions.

7 In the future, we will use electric cars.

4 GRAMMAR If we only cared a little bit more … ____/8

a) Complete the sentences with the correct form of the **if-clauses** type 1 or 2. (5P)

👉	If-Sätze – Conditional sentences (type 1 and 2)		
	Type 1	If-clause: **simple present**	Main clause: **will-future** **can/should/must + Infinitiv**
	Type 2	If-clause: **simple past**	Main clause: **would/could/might + Infinitiv**

1 The world _____ (be) much greener if we reduced our rubbish just a little bit.

2 If the heating of the atmosphere continues, more icebergs _____ (melt).

3 If more icebergs _____ (melt), the water level will rise.

4 People _____ (stop) destroying the environment if they just thought a little bit more.

5 We could help the environment a lot if we _____ (go) by bike instead of car.

b) Read the sentences and then circle the right answer. (3P)

1 If I took two-minute showers, I would help to save water.

   Do I help to save water?   Yes / No

2 If we go to school by bike, we will reduce our carbon footprint.

   Can we reduce our carbon footprint?   Yes / No

3 If our class decides to sort the garbage, we will be able to do something for the environment.

   Can we do something for the environment? Yes / No

MEDIATION

____ / 16

The Speed 'n' heat manual

Here is a part of a microwave instruction manual. Translate it into German.

> **Translation**
> Bei einer Übersetzung sollst du alle Informationen und Details eines (in diesem Fall technischen) Textes exakt in die Zielsprache übertragen. Nachdem du den ganzen Text einmal gelesen hast, beginnst du Satz für Satz mit deiner Übersetzung. Unbekannte Wörter kannst du am Ende im Wörterbuch nachschauen.
> Weitere Hinweise findest du im Skills File auf S. 146 in deinem Englischbuch.

Congratulations! You have bought the latest microwave oven.
Please read the following instructions carefully to fully enjoy your microwave.

Unpack your Microwave Oven

1. Carefully remove the appliance from the box. Remove all packaging materials from the inside of the microwave oven.

2. Carefully remove the clear plastic film on the control panel.

3. Check if there is any damage to the microwave, such as a broken door or damaged parts inside the appliance.

4. DO NOT USE IF THERE IS ANY DAMAGE!

Using the microwave

1. Set the required power and the time, then press 'Start'. At the end of the chosen time, the microwave stops automatically, and a beep sound will be heard.

2. Never use the oven if the turntable is not installed.

3. Never place the microwave upside down.

4. Never heat material not suitable for microwaves. This includes plastic, metallic things and pets.

SPEAKING

____/12

Drama instead of science?

Imagine your school wants to reduce the number of science lessons to make time for a new drama group. There is a lively discussion in your class about it. Now, it is your turn to deliver a speech on this topic.

Decide if you are for or against reducing the number of science lessons at your school. Deliver your speech and

- say why the number of science lessons should or should not be reduced at school,
- explain why we need or why we do not need science,
- give examples of why science, literature or theatre is important for our everyday lives.

You may take notes.

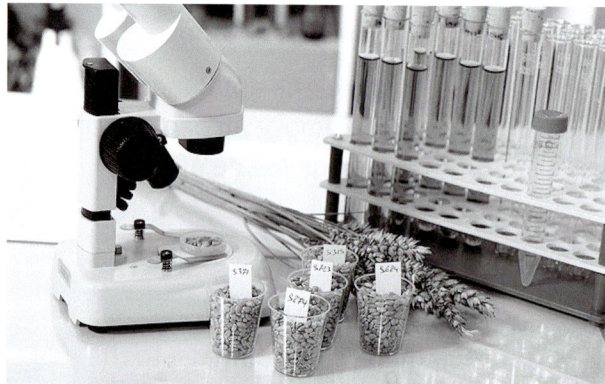

Klassenarbeit B

Unit 3

41

Gesamtpunktzahl _____ / 63   Note _____

LISTENING

_____ / 14

🎧 07 **A family discussion**

a) *Listen to the dialogue and tick the correct statements. (4P)*

1	Dad	a) tells his kids that he is going to sell the family car.	☐
		b) wants to make a difference and help the environment.	☐
		c) wants to get fit.	☐
		d) wants to go by bike.	☐

2	Sarah	a) sees a problem with the shopping.	☐
		b) is 17 years old.	☐
		c) wants to take a taxi to get home after a party.	☐
		d) wants to go on holiday by car.	☐

3	Sarah	a) doesn't like Chris's idea.	☐
		b) wants to have driving lessons with her father.	☐
		c) wants her father to give her a car as a birthday present.	☐
		d) worries that she won't be able to take all her suitcases with her when they go on holiday.	☐

4	Chris	a) likes his father's idea.	☐
		b) would like to use public transport.	☐
		c) wants to go on holidays by plane.	☐
		d) only has some information about another car sharing system.	☐

b) Who says what? Read the following statements and decide if they are part of Chris's or his father's idea for the car sharing system. Write the numbers of the statements under the correct photo. You may listen again. (10P)

Chris   **Dad**

_____   _____

1 In this system, you can register online.

2 In this system, you sell your own car.

3 In this system, people can rent your car.

4 In this system, you book a car on the internet.

5 In this system, you don't pay tax and insurance for the car.

6 In this system, you keep your own car.

7 In this system, you only pay when your car is rented by somebody.

8 In this system, the registration doesn't cost anything.

9 In this system, you become a member of the organization.

10 In this system, you set your own rates.

READING

/8

"Gattaca" – A film review

Read the text. Some parts are missing in it. Match the parts below to the text.

"Gattaca", written and directed by Andrew Niccols in 1997, is one of those films which is really worth watching. It tells a story about discrimination in the era of genetic engineering.

Jerome (Ethan Hawke) works for Gattaca, a space agency. In the morning, he prepares himself for work ❶. It seems that he has something to hide.

❷, we learn that Jerome is actually a man named Vincent Freeman. He was born the "natural way", needs glasses, ❸ and is only supposed to live to the age of 30. He doesn't fit in the world of perfect genetic humans like his younger brother Anton (Loren Dean) who ❹. As an adult, Vincent's job is to clean the rooms at Gattaca. As he dreams of taking part in a space mission, he swaps identities with Jerome Eugene Morrow (Jude Law), a perfect genetic human who is in a wheelchair after a car accident, and who has lost hope. Vincent alias Jerome ❺ to pass the gene tests at Gattaca in the morning.

Vincent ❻ and undergo many tests. Finally he gets permission to go on the space mission. But his program director is killed, and the police start their investigation. Will they find out his secret? Will he be able to go on the space mission?

Vincent, the actual loser in the perfect genetic world of Gattaca, ❼. That's the message of the film: there's no gene for the human spirit.

The beautiful pictures and the wonderful music are what make the film so special. It shows possible life in the future and gives the audience the chance to think about the advantages and disadvantages of such a perfect genetic world. The film even gives detailed pictures about genetic manipulation. To give an example, when Vincent is at a classical music concert, the pianist has twelve fingers. This is not shown by any special effects, but by the glove that Vincent catches and by the promotional poster outside of the hall. And that a future like this may not be too far away ❽ in our world, too.

A	has heart problems
B	has to train hard
C	in an extensive flashback
D	in a strange way
E	never gives up and fights for his dream
F	is shown by the fact that there has been successful cloning
G	starts to use tiny bits of Jerome's hair, blood, skin and urine
H	was perfectioned via genetic manipulation while still an embryo

Unit 3 | Klassenarbeit B

LANGUAGE

___/ 15

1 WORDS Phrasal verbs

___/ 9

a) *Re-write the following sentences using a **phrasal verb** instead of the underlined words. (5P)*

1 Suddenly the fire alarm <u>started</u>.

2 If you don't <u>lower</u> the volume, I will become deaf.

3 <u>Be quick</u>! It's time to go to school.

4 If we <u>continue</u> like this, our children will have a bad future.

5 Please <u>check</u> if we have enough money for the trip.

b) *Now re-write the following sentences in a more formal style, i.e. without phrasal verbs. (4P)*

1 Bill <u>asked</u> her <u>out</u> on a date.

2 You shouldn't <u>put on</u> jeans for your job interview.

3 Could you <u>work out</u> how much I have to pay, please?

4 Janet <u>broke up</u> with John because she had found another man.

2 WORDS Our perfect future world

____/6

Complete the sentences with words from the box. Make sure you use the correct form of the words.
Be careful: there are three more words than you need.

> (to) aid • (to) calculate • feature • (to) investigate • message •
> (to) recommend • robot • sensible • volume

In the future, _____ will do all the housework for us. But they will have a lot more

great _____. For example, they will cook for us and _____ the

perfect food. They will tell us to be _____ about our health. They will be able to

_____ us to watch our weight by _____ how much we are

allowed to eat and will keep food away from us. Maybe it is not so good to have a robot influencing our

lives like that …

WRITING

____/10

A film review

Write a review of a film you have seen recently. It can be either one you liked or one you completely disliked.
Write between 180 and 200 words in your exercise book.

> **A film review**
> ☐ Deine Filmbesprechung sollte dem Leser / der Leserin einen Überblick über das Wesentliche des Films verschaffen.
> ☐ Hierzu zählen der Inhalt des Films, die Namen der (Haupt-)Darsteller / Darstellerinnen und evtl. des Regisseurs / der Regisseurin.
> ☐ Das Ende solltest du jedoch offen lassen.
> ☐ Gib außerdem an, was die Botschaft des Films ist und ob er dir gefallen hat oder nicht.
> Weitere Hinweise findest du im Skills File auf S. 156 in deinem Englischbuch.

STUDY SKILLS

____/ 16

Giving a group presentation

a) Look at the following sentences that could be said in a group presentation about environment protection and put them into a suitable order. (8P)

	A	So, we'll come to the end. Let me sum up.
	B	Thanks for listening. Have you got any questions?
	C	Finally, let's talk about the consequences. One of the main consequences is dying nature.
	D	Good morning. Everybody should help to save our environment today. We are going to tell you now how we can all contribute.
	E	In the first part, I would like to tell you about how and why our earth is being polluted.
	F	We've divided our presentation into three parts. Ethan will first talk about reasons for environmental pollution. Next Sam will look at what that means for our earth. Last but not least, Charlie will show you what we can all do about it.
	G	Okay, I think it's time to come to the end.
	H	If there aren't any questions, thanks very much for your attention.

b) Now match the sentences to the different roles (team leader, co-leader and presenter) in a group presentation. Write the sentence number into the correct box. Be careful: there can be more than one role for a sentence. (8P)

Team-leader	Co-leader	Presenter

Klassenarbeit A

Unit 4

47

Gesamtpunktzahl ohne Speaking _____ / 70   Note _____

LISTENING

_____ / 18

Coffee talk about books and films

🎧 08 **a)** *Josie and Adam are talking about books and films. Listen to the first part of the conversation and answer the questions. You don't have to write complete sentences. (12P)*

1. What does Adam not like about the film? *(3 facts)*

   _____
   _____
   _____

2. Why does Josie prefer watching films to reading books? *(3 facts)*

   _____
   _____
   _____

3. What does Adam think is brilliant about books? *(3 facts)*

   _____
   _____
   _____

4. What does Josie think makes a film more exciting? *(2 facts)*

   _____
   _____

5. How has Adam been affected by imagining things while reading?

   _____

🎧 09 **b)** *Listen to the second part of the dialogue. Put the sentences in the correct order. (6P)*

	A	Adam says it can be disappointing that important parts of the book are missing in the film.
	B	Adam thinks you do something for your brain while reading.
	C	Josie says films can show how people lived in the past and what other places on earth look like.
	D	Josie says they're never going to agree completely.
	E	Adam doesn't like the fact that in film adaptations so many things are different to the book.
	F	Josie thinks films make it easier to understand the classics.

LANGUAGE

____ / 32

1 WORDS About novels and short stories

____ / 8

Complete the sentences with the correct literary term.

1. A _____ tells the story from his/her own perspective; this means he/she has a limited point of view.

2. A narrator who knows everything about every character tells the story from an _____.

3. Short stories may have a clear beginning, a _____ and a resolution.

4. A person in a story is a _____.

5. Short stories usually focus on a single setting while novels can be _____ different times and places.

6. Modern short stories may end in two different ways. They can have a _____ or be _____.

7. A long fictional text that has different characters, action and, usually, a plot is called a _____.

2 WORDS I love reading Charles Dickens

____ / 9

Complete the sentences with words from the box. Be careful: there are two more than you need.

> (to) await • (to) bother • classic • curious • impression • (to) intend •
> memorable • moving • (to) request • suitcase • thus

Lately, I found a book in an old _____ in the garage. It was an old edition of

a _____. I started to read it; it was really _____.

"Oliver Twist" by Charles Dickens is a _____ book.

While reading I was always _____ about what

_____ him on his journey. _____,

I bought another novel by Charles Dickens which also made a great

_____ on me, "Great Expectations". I like the way

Dickens writes his books and I _____ to read all his novels.

3 GRAMMAR REVISION+ Brave Little Red Riding Hood

_____/9

Write down the following dialogue in indirect speech.

☞ **Die indirekte Rede**
Steht das einleitende Verb der indirekten Rede im **simple past** (z.B. *said, told, ...*), werden die Zeiten der direkten Rede in der Regel um eine Zeitstufe in die Vergangenheit gesetzt.

Direct speech	Indirect speech
Present	Past
Past	Past perfect
Present perfect	Past perfect
Past perfect	Past perfect
Will-future	Would + infinitive
Going-to-future	Was/were going to + infinitve

Beachte außerdem, dass sich die Pronomen ändern, je nachdem, wer die direkte Rede geäußert hat.
Weitere Hinweise findest du im Grammar File 8 auf S. 184–185 in deinem Englischbuch.

1 The wolf: "I will go to grandma's house, eat her and wait for Little Red Riding Hood."

   The wolf thought _____.

2 Little Red Riding Hood: "Grandma, you have such big eyes!"

   Little Red Riding Hood said _____.

3 The wolf: "Yes, so I can see you better."

   The wolf answered _____.

4 Little Red Riding Hood: "You aren't my grandma, you are the wolf. You want to eat me too."

   Little Red Riding Hood shouted _____.

5 The wolf: "What are you doing with the knife?"

   The wolf wanted to know _____.

6 Little Red Riding Hood: "I want to free my grandma who you ate before I came."

   Little Red Riding Hood explained _____.

7 Grandma: "I'm so happy that you helped me. I can't believe that the wolf ate me."

   Grandma said _____.

8 Little Red Riding Hood: "Last year I read that wolves like eating grandmas."

   Little Red Riding Hood said _____.

9 Grandma: "Are you going to visit me again soon?"

   Grandma wanted to know whether _____.

4 GRAMMAR REVISION+ Who, which, that or nothing at all?   ___/6

*Lisa has to write an essay about her experience reading the book "The absolutely true diary of a part-time Indian". Tick the correct **relative pronoun** or **pronouns**. Also tick "not necessary" when you can leave the relative pronoun out.*

		who	which	that	not necessary
1	Usually I don't like the books _____ we read in the lessons very much.	☐	☐	☐	☐
2	But I really like this book _____ is about a young Indian living on a reservation.	☐	☐	☐	☐
3	A Native American _____ I met in the hotel lobby during my last holidays in the USA told me a lot about Indian tribes.	☐	☐	☐	☐
4	I have to find out whether there is a film _____ deals with the topic of the book.	☐	☐	☐	☐
5	I have already seen a film _____ was based on a book, and that was really good.	☐	☐	☐	☐
6	The Last of the Mohicans is the next book _____ I am going to read.	☐	☐	☐	☐

WRITING

____/ 20

A book report

Write an article for your English partner school's magazine about the excerpt from the book "Looking for Alaska" by John Green in your English book on pp. 77–83. Tell your readers why you think they should or shouldn't read the whole book. Write about 200 words.

 Eine Buchbesprechung
- In einer Buchbesprechung gibst du die wichtigsten Daten, den Inhalt und deine eigene Einschätzung zum Buch wieder.
- Beginne deine Besprechung mit der Nennung des Autors / der Autorin, Titels und Genre des Buches. Du kannst auch mit einem interessanten Zitat aus dem Buch einsteigen, um die Aufmerksamkeit deiner Leser / Leserinnen zu wecken.
- Dann gibst du eine kurze inhaltliche Zusammenfassung des Buches, ohne jedoch das Ende zu verraten.
- Abschließend schilderst du deine eigene Meinung zum Buch und sagst, warum du das Buch zum Lesen empfiehlst oder nicht.

Unit 4 — Klassenarbeit B

Gesamtpunktzahl ohne Speaking _____ / 54   Note _____

Gesamtpunktzahl mit Speaking _____ / 66   Note _____

READING _____ /5

Ex Poser

Ex Poser By Paul Jennings

There are two rich kids in our form. Sandra Morris and Ben Fox. They are both snobs. They think they are too good for the rest of us. Their parents have big cars and big houses. Both of them are quiet. They keep to themselves. I guess they don't want to mix with the ruffians[1] like me.

Ben Fox always wears expensive gym shoes and the latest fashions. He thinks he is good-looking with his blue eyes and blond hair. He is a real poser.

Sandra Morris is the same. And she knows it. Blue eyes and blonde hair too. Skin like silk. Why do some kids get the best of everything?

Me, I landed pimples[2]. I've used everything I can on them. But still they bud and grow and burst. Just when you don't want them to. It's not fair.

Anyway, today I have the chance to even things up. Boffin is bringing along his latest invention – a lie detector. Sandra Morris is the victim. She agreed to try it out because everyone knows that she would never tell a lie. What she doesn't know is that Boffin and I are going to ask her some very embarrassing questions.

Boffin is a brain. His inventions always work. He is smarter than the teachers. Everyone knows that. And now he has brought along his latest effort[3]. A lie detector.

He tapes two wires[4] to Sandra's arm. 'It doesn't hurt,' he says. 'But it is deadly accurate.' He switches on the machine and a little needle swings into the middle of the dial. 'Here's a trial question,' he says. 'Are you a girl?' Sandra nods.

'You have to say yes or no,' he says.

'Yes,' replies Sandra. The needle swings over to TRUTH. Maybe this thing really works. Boffin gives a big grin.

'This time tell a lie.' says Boffin. 'Are you a girl?' he asks again.

Sandra smiles with that lovely smile of hers. 'No,' she says. A little laugh goes up but then all the kids in the room gasp. The needle points to LIE. This lie detector is a terrific[5] invention!

'OK,' says Boffin. 'You only have seven questions, David. The batteries will go flat after another seven questions.' He sits down behind his machine and twiddles the knobs.

This is going to be fun. I am going to find out a little bit about Sandra Morris and Ben Fox. It's going to be very interesting. Very interesting indeed.

I ask my first question. 'Have you ever kissed Ben Fox?'

Sandra goes red. Ben Fox goes red. I have got them this time. I am sure they have something going between them. I will expose[6] them.

'No,' says Sandra. Everyone cranes their neck to see what the lie detector says. The needle points to TRUTH.

This is not what I expected. And I only have six questions left. I can't let her off the hook. I am going to expose them both.

'Have you ever held his hand?'

Again she says, 'No.' And the needle says TRUTH. I am starting to feel guilty. Why am I doing this?

I try another tack[7]. 'Are you in love?' I ask.

A red flush starts to crawl up her neck. I am feeling really mean now. Fox is blushing[8] like a sunset.

'Yes,' she says. The needle points to TRUTH.

---

[1] ruffian ['rʌfiən] *Grobian*   [2] pimple ['pɪmpl] *Pustel*   [3] effort ['efət] *hier: Versuch*   [4] wire ['waɪə(r)] *Draht*
[5] terrific [tə'rɪfɪk] *fantastisch*   [6] expose [ɪk'spəʊz] *bloßstellen*   [7] tack [tæk] *Richtung*   [8] blush [blʌʃ] *erröten*

I shouldn't have let the kids talk me into doing this. I decide to put Sandra and Ben out of their agony[9]. I won't actually name him. I'll spare[10] her that. 'Is he in this room?' I say.
She looks at the red Ben Fox. 'Yes,' she says. The needle points to TRUTH.
'Has he got blue eyes?' I ask.
'No,' she says.
'Brown?' I say.
'No,' she says again.
I don't know what to say next. I look at each kid in the class very carefully. Ben Fox has blue eyes. I was sure that she loved him.
'This thing doesn't work,' I say to Boffin. 'I can't see one kid who doesn't have either blue eyes or brown eyes.'
'We can,' says Boffin. They are all looking at me.
I can feel my face turning red now. I wish I could sink through the floor but I get on with my last question.
'Is he an idiot?' I ask.
Sandra is very embarrassed. 'Yes,' she says in a voice that is softer than a whisper. 'And he has green eyes.'

Read the text carefully and tick the correct ending.

1	The narrator thinks that	a) Sandra and Ben don't want to talk to other students.	
		b) Sandra and Ben don't want to be seen with other students.	
		c) Sandra and Ben don't want to mix with him.	

2	The narrator is jealous of	a) Sandra's and Ben's nice behaviour.	
		b) Sandra's and Ben's lives.	
		c) Sandra's and Ben's perfect skin.	

3	The narrator asks Sandra personal questions	a) to make her embarrassed.	
		b) to show how arrogant she is.	
		c) to make fun of her.	

4	The narrator wants to	a) test Sandra about her love life.	
		b) test Sandra about her relationships.	
		c) test Sandra about her relationship to Ben.	

5	At the end he learns that Sandra	a) has fallen in love with his friend Boffin.	
		b) has fallen in love with him.	
		c) has fallen in love with Ben.	

[9] agony ['ægəni] *Qual*   [10] spare [speə(r)] *ersparen*

LANGUAGE

___/ 37

1 WORDS A literature crossword

___/ 14

Complete the crossword with the correct words.

Across

1. a scene that goes back in time and shows what happened earlier than the main story and is often shown as a memory
4. language that uses images to produce a certain picture in mind
5. an important idea that is transported
10. a person who tells the story
12. the sequence of events of a story
13. an imagined piece of literature
14. the time and place the story happens

Down

2. a writer of a book
3. a certain mood in which a piece of literature is set
6. creation of excitement or fear during a story
7. the main controversy between different characters in a piece of literature
8. a short part taken from a book
9. a synonym for 'song text'
11. a report discussing a piece of literature

2 WORDS Guess what it is! ____/ 14

a) Match the following definitions to the correct stylistic device from the box. *(7P)*

| alliteration • irony • metaphor • personification • rhyme • simile • symbol |

1 Expressing the opposite of what you really mean, often in a humorous way. _____

2 Repetition of the same letter or sound at the beginning of neighbouring words. _____

3 Using words with the same sound especially at the end of lines in a poem or song. _____

4 An object that stands for an idea. _____

5 Comparison between two seemingly unlike things that have something in common. The poet talks about it as if it is something else. _____

6 Representing something, for example an object as human. _____

7 Something is compared to something else with 'like' or 'as'. _____

b) Now match the stylistic devices from *a)* to the correct example. *(7P)*

A Money makes me mad. _____

B You dropped the glass – clever! _____

C An apple a day keeps the doctor away. _____

D What a stupid computer! It's shutting down again. _____

E His home was a prison to him. _____

F A lion stands for strength. _____

G She was as cold as ice. _____

Unit 4 | Klassenarbeit B

3 GRAMMAR REVISION+ How to put the world on a stage

___/9

Two drama students are talking about aspects of theatre productions.
*Write what they say using **gerunds**.*

2 interpret – dialogues – is necessary – to understand the plot

3 put – your own understanding of a book – into the play – can improve it

1 speak – clearly – is very important – for good actors

4 nevertheless – pay respect to – stage directions – is required

5 be – very nervous – shortly before a performance – is normal

6 you should not mind – get bad reviews

7 have – a good imagination – helps you to perform a play

8 an actor or an actress – isn't able to act – without learn – the text of his/her role

9 you should be interested in – sing and dance

10 to be able to – act successfully – rehearse a lot – is essential

1 *Speaking clearly is very important for good actors.*

2 _____

3 _____

4 _____

5 _____

6 _____

7 _____

8 _____

9 _____

10 _____

MEDIATION

___/12

"Fairytaleheart" – A review

You talked to your English penfriend lately about the theatre. Now, you have been to "Fairytaleheart" by Philip Ridley and want to recommend this play to him/her.

Read the text below and explain in English to your penfriend why he/she should watch the play. Write him/her an e-mail.

Fairytaleheart

„Fairytaleheart" (dt. Märchenherz) ist ein einaktiges Theaterstück mit nur zwei Figuren. Es spielt im Londoner East End.

Eines Abends im Winter treffen Kirsty und Gideon im ehemaligen, verlassenen Gemeindezentrum aufeinander. Kirsty, die den Tod ihrer Mutter noch nicht verarbeitet hat, ist von zuhause abgehauen, nachdem sie erfahren hat, dass ihr Vater wieder heiraten will. Im Gemeindezentrum trifft sie auf Gideon, der allein bei seiner Hippie-Mutter aufgewachsen ist und seinen Vater nicht kennt. Gideon hat sich im Gemeindezentrum eine traumhafte bunte Landschaft gemalt.

Wie es seine Mutter mit ihm gemacht hat, nimmt Gideon Kirsty inmitten von Kerzen und wunderschönen bunten Bildern mit auf eine fantastische Reise. Gideon hat so gelernt, sich selbst zu beschützen und Trost zu geben und auch Kirsty beginnt, die Dinge anders zu sehen.

Die Geschichte mag ein wenig einfach konstruiert und die Charaktere wenig bedeutsam erscheinen, aber die Handlung trifft genau auf den Punkt und konfrontiert das jugendliche Publikum mit seinen eigenen Problemen.

SPEAKING

/12

A poem

"What lips my lips have kissed, and where, and why"

By Edna St Vincent Millay (1892–1950)

What lips my lips have kissed, and where, and why,
I have forgotten, and what arms have lain
Under my head till morning; but the rain
Is full of ghosts tonight, that tap and sigh[1]
5   Upon[2] the glass and listen for reply;
And in my heart there stirs[3] a quiet pain
For unremembered lads[4] that not again
Will turn to me at midnight[5] with a cry.
Thus in the winter stands the lonely tree,
10 Nor[6] knows what birds have vanished[7] one by one,
Yet knows its boughs[8] more silent than before:
I cannot say what loves have come and gone;
I only know that summer sang in me
A little while, that in me sings no more.

Read the text aloud. Think about which words you want to stress and when you should make a pause.

Talk about the poem. You should

- describe what the poem is about,
- describe the rhyme scheme,
- explain what imagery Millay uses in lines 9 to 14 and what it is about,
- explain the metaphor in lines 9 to 10,
- say if you like the poem or not and why.

Make sure your talk has an introduction and a conclusion.

You may make notes first.

---

[1] sigh [saɪ] *seufzen*   [2] upon [əˈpɒn] *auf*   [3] stir [stɜː(r)] *sich rühren*   [4] lad [læd] *Kerl*
[5] midnight [ˈmɪdnaɪt] *Mitternacht*   [6] nor [nɔː(r)] *auch nicht*   [7] vanish [ˈvænɪʃ] *verschwinden*   [8] bough [baʊ] *Zweig*

How to do well in a test

Countdown zum Testerfolg

Ein Test ist angekündigt? Kein Grund zur Panik. Wichtig ist, dass du weißt, worauf du dich vorbereiten musst. Im Zweifelsfall frag deine Lehrerin oder deinen Lehrer. Der Countdown kann beginnen!

Eine Woche vor dem Test

1. Lies noch einmal die **Texte** der zuletzt durchgenommenen Unit (Parts A, B, C, D). Fasse mündlich oder schriftlich zusammen, worum es ging.
2. Wiederhole den **Wortschatz** der Unit mit Hilfe des *Vocabulary* oder des *Wordmaster*. Schreibe dir die Wörter und Wortverbindungen, die du immer wieder vergisst, auf ein Blatt Papier. Eine Mindmap oder ein Wortfeld helfen beim Behalten.
3. Geh auch noch mal die neue **Grammatik** durch. Aufgaben zur Selbstüberprüfung und zum Üben findest du im *Practice*-Teil, auf den Seiten „Revision – Getting ready for a test", im *Grammar File* (S. 165–196), ,in deinem *Workbook* und im *e-Workbook*.

Zwei Tage vor dem Test

1. Wiederhole den **Wortschatz**. Manche Wörter sitzen noch nicht? Schreibe einen kurzen Text, in dem du sie verwendest.
2. Lies die **Texte** ein weiteres Mal.
3. Erkläre einem Freund oder einer Freundin die neue **Grammatik**. Das klappt nicht richtig? Dann lies nochmal im *Grammar File* nach.

Am Abend vor dem Test

1. Entspanne dich. Du kannst lesen, dich in die Badewanne legen, Musik hören, fernsehen, …
2. Geh zur gewohnten Zeit ins Bett.

Am Morgen des Tests

1. Steh rechtzeitig auf, damit du nicht hetzen musst.
2. Lies irgendetwas „zum Aufwärmen", aber schau nicht mehr in dein Schülerbuch.

Während des Tests

1. Denk daran: Du hast dich gut vorbereitet. Es gibt keinen Grund, nervös zu sein.
2. Konzentriere dich auf den Test, lass dich nicht ablenken.
3. Lies dir die Aufgaben genau durch. Dann löse zuerst die Aufgaben, die dir einfach scheinen. Wende dich erst danach den schwereren Aufgaben zu.
4. Aufgaben, die du bearbeitet hast, hakst du ab. So siehst du, wie du vorankommst, und behältst den Überblick.
5. Schau ab und zu auf die Uhr. Du solltest dir für den Schluss noch etwas Zeit einplanen, um deine Antworten noch einmal durchzulesen und wenn nötig zu korrigieren.

Aufgabenstellungen verstehen

Bevor du anfängst, die Aufgaben zu bearbeiten, vergewissere dich, dass du genau weißt, was du tun sollst. Lies die Aufgabe Wort für Wort langsam und gründlich und von Anfang bis Ende durch. Du kannst besonders wichtige Teile der Aufgabenstellung unterstreichen und die Aufgabe, wenn nötig, für dich in einzelne Schritte unterteilen.

Den folgenden Arbeitsanweisungen begegnest du häufig:

Add	Verbinde eine Information oder einen Sachverhalt mit einer/einem anderen auf die geforderte Art und Weise.
Choose	Wähle zwischen verschiedenen Möglichkeiten die passende Information aus.
Comment	Kommentiere einen Sachverhalt durch die Darstellung deiner eigenen Meinung dazu. Begründe und erläutere sie möglichst genau.
Compare	Vergleiche Dinge, Wörter oder Sachverhalte, indem du prüfst, ob und auf welche Weise sie gleiche oder verschiedene Eigenschaften, Aussehen, Bedeutungen oder Funktionen haben.
Complete	Ergänze eine Information, indem du sie an dem dafür vorgesehenen Platz einträgst und damit z. B. einen Satz sinnvoll beendest.
Describe	Beschreibe ein Objekt oder eine Person, d.h. stelle dar, wie sie aussehen, wie das Objekt funktioniert oder die Personen handeln. Vermeide eigene Wertungen wie z. B. „beautiful", „useful" oder „great".
Discuss	Diskutiere ein Thema, eine Behauptung oder eine Aussage. Untersuche möglichst viele Seiten davon, z. B. Vor- und Nachteile, und stelle diese geordnet dar.
Explain	Erkläre einen Sachverhalt, d. h. gib wesentliche Fakten über ihn und erläutere, wie sie logisch zusammenhängen.
Fill in	Trage die geforderten Informationen in den dafür vorgesehenen Platz ein, z. B. in eine Lücke oder eine Tabelle.
List	Schreibe einzelne oder mehrere Informationen übersichtlich und geordnet auf, z. B. in einer Reihe, Tabelle oder einem anderen Verzeichnis.
Listen	Höre dir einen Text, einzelne Informationen oder Sachverhalte an.
Match	Ordne die angegebenen Informationen einander zu, wie es die Aufgabe erfordert. Finde z. B. Satzanfänge und passende Satzenden und füge sie zusammen.
Use	Verwende eine Tatsache, ein Wort usw. so, wie es in der Aufgabe gefordert wird.
Write a ...	Schreibe etwas in einem geforderten Textformat auf, z. B. deinen Kommentar zu etwas oder eine Geschichte.